Sid and Nim

by Tim Little

Illustrated by Emma Levey

Kit

Pip

Nim

OXFORD

UNIVERSITY PRESS

Sid is sad.

Sid

Dad

Pip spots Sid and his dad on the other side of the street. They are putting up a poster.

Pip and Kit are looking at a <u>sign</u> that tells them a guinea pig called Nim is missing. Can you point to the <u>sign</u>?

Pip and Kit set out to look for Nim.

Pip!

Kit is trying to get Pip's <u>attention</u>. It means he wants her to listen to him. Why do you think Kit is trying to do this?

7

It is Nim!

Nim is stuck in the fence! Why is it <u>important</u> that Pip and Kit help Nim?

mat

Pip and Kit <u>return</u> Nim. Does that mean that they give him back or that they keep him?

Sid pats Nim.
Nim naps.

What happened to Nim?

Can you make up your own story about how Nim got stuck in the hole? The images below might help you.